AMAZING
WORD
POWER

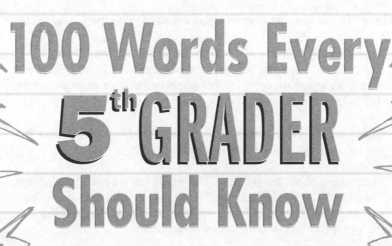

100 Words Every 5th GRADER Should Know

New York • Toronto • London • Auckland • Sydney
Mexico City • New Delhi • Hong Kong • Buenos Aires

Welcome to Amazing Word Power!

By picking up this book you've entered the world of Amazing Words. And you're on your way to building your own Amazing Word Power.

There are 100 great words in this book. Some you may know already. Some may look familiar. But many of them are meant to challenge you! The illustrations and easy-to-understand definitions will help you to learn and remember them.

Ready? Before you get started, you may want to do the following:

1. Use the Checklist that starts on page 125 along with the back cover flap to see what words you know and don't know. (Be sure to use a dry-erase marker.) Do this again in a couple of weeks. This will help you keep track of your growing word power.

2. Check out the Word Power Tips on page 124. Following these tips will help you boost your word learning.

3. Learn more about the words. Many words have several definitions. We didn't include all these definitions, but you can find them—as well as information about the origins of the words—by looking in a dictionary or searching in an online dictionary.

4. Have fun!

Contents

1

reminisce

(*rem*-uh-**niss**) verb

grandpa loves to reminisce about the good old days.

What It Means

To think or talk about the past and things that you remember

How to Use It

My mother likes to *reminisce* about her childhood.

More About It

⊜ *Synonym* remember

conclude

(kuhn-**klood**) verb

What It Means

To arrive at a decision or realization based on the facts that you have

How to Use It

Given the evidence, we can only *conclude* that he is guilty.

More About It

⊜ *Synonym* infer

Stop yelling! I get it. I conclude that you're in a bad mood.

3

contemplate

(**kon**-tuhm-plate) verb

What It Means

To think seriously about something

How to Use It

My mother always says, "Don't *contemplate* cleaning your room. Just do it."

More About It

● *Synonym*   consider

Maybe I'll pick up my socks . . .

My stomach hurts, but I'm <u>contemplating</u> eating another doughnut. Help!

prognosticate

(*prog*-**noss**-tuh-kate) verb

What It Means

To make a guess about the future

How to Use It

The fortune teller promised to *prognosticate* about our future.

More About It

 *Related word* prognosis

Our coach prognosticates that we will win on Saturday.

5

mnemonic

(nee-**mon**-ik) noun

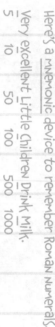

What It Means

A word, poem, sentence, or picture that helps you remember something

How to Use It

The *mnemonic* HOMES helps me remember the names of the Great Lakes.

More About It

The first "m" in *mnemonic* is silent.

Here's a mnemonic device to remember Roman numerals.
Very excellent Little Children Drink Milk.
5 10 50 100 500 1000

Activity Sheet

Read each clue. Then write the answers in the spiral puzzle.

1. To use facts to make a decision

2. What weather reporters try to do

3. An aid to help you remember something

4. Something you should do before you spend your whole allowance!

5. Photographs, home videos, and scrapbooks can help people do this.

		2.				
		4.				
		5.				
1.			3.			

START

6

avert

(uh-**vurt**) verb

Roscoe averted an accident by making a sharp turn on his bike.

What It Means

To turn away or to prevent

How to Use It

We all *averted* our eyes when the teacher called for volunteers.

More About It

Related word   aversion

Who wants to read their report first?

inadvertently

(in-ad-**vur**-tuhnt-lee) adverb

What It Means

Not on purpose; mistakenly

How to Use It

The driver told the police officer he had *inadvertently* gone too fast.

More About It

⊜ *Synonym* accidentally

I inadvertently put my left shoe on my right foot. Oops!

diversion

(di-**vur**-zhuhn) noun

Favorite fun diversions: eating, e-mailing, reminiscing, watching movies, did I mention eating...?

What It Means

Something that takes your mind off other things

How to Use It

Sam's favorite *diversion* is playing baseball.

More About It

= *Synonym*   entertainment

introvert

(**in**-truh-vurt) noun

What It Means

Someone who is shy and keeps his or her thoughts and feelings from others

How to Use It

Juan is an *introvert*. He hardly talks to anyone

More About It

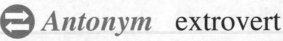 ***Antonym*** extrovert

Can a BIG MOUTH like me be an *introvert*?

YES. Now leave me alone!

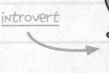

introvert

10

convert

(kuhn-**vurt**) verb

What It Means

To switch from one belief or idea to another one; to change a thing into something else

How to Use It

The huge sundae *converted* Tiffany into a dessert fan.

More About It

= *Synonym*   change

My mom said if we could convert my excuses into cash, we'd be rich. Very funny.

Activity Sheet

What word can help you remember the meaning of the Latin root *ver* or *vert*? Use the clues to fill in the correct words below. Then write the boxed letters at the bottom of the page.

1. Someone who is very shy
2. What many people hope diversions will provide
3. To turn away from something
4. To switch from one idea to another
5. Something that takes your mind off other things
6. A synonym for *accidentally*

1. _ _ □ _ _ _ _ _ _

2. _ □ _

3. _ _ _ □ _

4. _ _ □ _ _ _

5. _ _ _ □ _ _

6. _ _ □ _ _ _ _ _ _

When you see the Latin root *ver* or *vert*, think of someone or something that has

‾ ‾ ‾ ‾ ‾ ‾ .
1 2 3 4 5 6

affluent

(af-loo-uhnt) adjective

What It Means

Lots of money = affluent.
No money = bankrupt.

Having plenty of money; rich

How to Use It

I like to see the mansions in the *affluent* part of town.

More About It

= *Synonym* wealthy

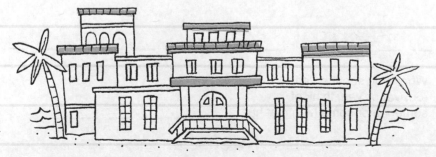

lucrative

(loo-kruh-tiv) adjective

What It Means

Well-paying or profitable

How to Use It

Krystal's summer job was very, very *lucrative*.

It's too bad that eating potato chips isn't <u>lucrative</u>. I'd be rich!

More About It

= *Synonym* gainful

$$$

asset

(as-set) noun

My assets for the lunch swap? 3 cookies and string cheese.

What It Means

A thing that a person or company owns

How to Use It

My iPod is my most prized *asset*.

More About It

 **Antonym** liability

This is my yummiest asset!

liability

(lye-uh-**bil**-i-tee) noun

What It Means

The money a person or company owes; a disadvantage

How to Use It

Anton never borrows money because he doesn't like having any *liabilities*.

More About It

⇄ *Antonym*   asset

Hmm . . . our guard dog loves everyone. That's a liability!

YOU OWE

15

diversify

(di-**vur**-suh-fye) verb

we always go to the same restaurant. Let's diversify.

What It Means

To be involved with a variety of things

How to Use It

The old surfboard company decided to *diversify* and sell skateboards, too.

More About It

⇄ *Antonym*   concentrate

Activity Sheet

Read each clue. Then write the answers in the spiral puzzle.

1. A synonym for *affluent*
2. Well-paying or profitable
3. A thing that a person or company owns
4. What all these words are about
5. The money a person or company owes
6. A synonym for *wealthy*
7. If you get involved in a variety of things, you _____ .

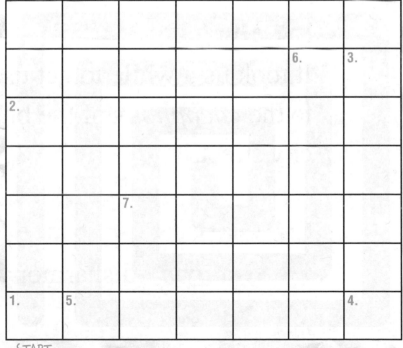

16

cacophony

(kuh-**ka**-fuh-*nee*) noun

Dad says my drum playing is a cacophony.

What It Means

A harsh, unpleasant sound or combination of sounds

How to Use It

It took us a while to get used to the *cacophony* of the busy city streets.

More About It

= *Synonym* disharmony

Rat-a-tat-tat!   ZOOM!   "Come back with that!"

"La, la, la, la . . ."   Bank   Beep! Beep!   "Hot dogs here!"

din

(**din**) noun

Ding! Ding! Ding!

What It Means

A great deal of noise

How to Use It

The *din* of the cuckoo clock woke us all up.

More About It

⊜ *Synonym*   clamor

Dina used earplugs to avoid the din of the rock concert.

Cuckoo! Cuckoo! Cuckoo! Cuckoo! Cuckoo! Cuckoo!

bellow

(**bel**-oh) verb

Hey, fellow. Mellow out. No need to bellow.

What It Means

To shout or to yell

How to Use It

Bob doesn't like it when Kailah *bellows* at him.

More About It

⊜ *Synonym*   roar

She can really bellow.

It ain't Bingo night until she bellows.

Bingo

raucous

(**raw**-kuhss) adjective

What It Means

Rough or loud

How to Use It

The *raucous* singer
was extremely popular.

More About It

 *Synonym* harsh

you like *raucous* rock n' roll. I like hopping hip-hop.

raucous rock n' roller

melodious

(muh-**loh**-dee-uhss) adjective

Hi, birdie. You have quite a melodious chirp.

What It Means

Pleasant to hear

How to Use It

Our plumber is very talented. He sings in a *melodious* voice while he works.

More About It

⊜ *Synonym*　tuneful

Oh faucet . . . you have such a melodious drip.

Activity Sheet

What animal makes the loudest sound? To find out, color in any space that contains two words that are synonyms. Some words come from earlier sections of this book.

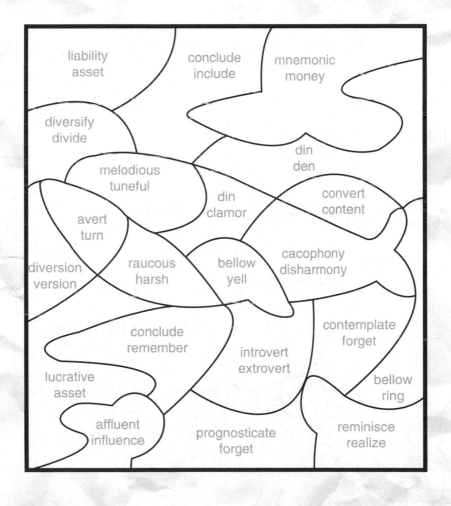

liability / asset

conclude / include

mnemonic / money

diversify / divide

din / den

melodious / tuneful

din / clamor

convert / content

avert / turn

diversion / version

raucous / harsh

bellow / yell

cacophony / disharmony

conclude / remember

contemplate / forget

lucrative / asset

introvert / extrovert

bellow / ring

affluent / influence

prognosticate / forget

reminisce / realize

nefarious

(ni-**fair**-ee-uhss) adjective

What It Means

Corrupt and vicious

How to Use It

The *nefarious* man frightened everyone he met.

More About It

 = *Synonym*   villainous

Mmuua-ha-ha-ha! After I release this concoction, they'll see who's the most nefarious of all!

infamous

(**in**-fuh-muhss) adjective

Uncle Ricky is infamous for telling looooong, booooooring stories.

What It Means

Having a bad reputation

How to Use It

Jesse James robbed so many banks that he became *infamous* around the country.

More About It

⊜ *Synonym*   notorious

infamous dude

heinous

(**hay**-nuhss) adjective

She made you eat liver? Heinous!!

What It Means

Terrible and shocking

How to Use It

The crime was so *heinous* even the police were shocked.

More About It

⊜ *Synonym*   monstrous

That was a <u>heinous</u> movie!

sublime

(suh-**blime**) adjective

What It Means

Amazingly wonderful

How to Use It

The weather on the island was *sublime*.

More About It

⊜ *Synonym* splendid

To rhyme is sublime.
You should try it sometime.

eminent

(em-uh-nuhnt) adjective

I love to build and hope to become an eminent architect.

What It Means

Well-known and respected

How to Use It

The soldier was the town's most *eminent* resident.

More About It

⊜ *Synonym*   famous

Activity Sheet

Play the game of Out and Over. Find a word in Box 1 that does not have the same meaning as the other three words. Move that word to Box 2 by writing it on the blank line. Continue until you reach Box 8. Then complete the sentence in that box.

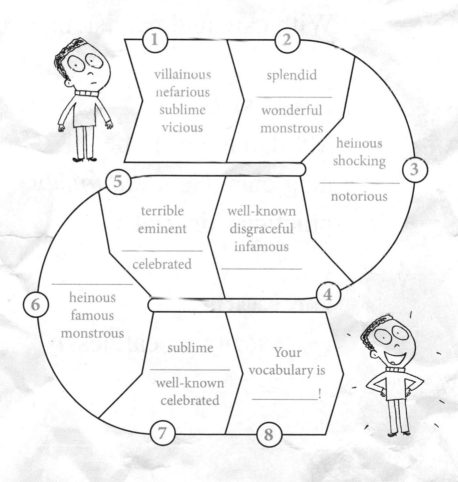

1
villainous
nefarious
sublime
vicious

2
splendid
_____
wonderful
monstrous

3
heinous
shocking
_____
notorious

5
terrible
eminent
_____
celebrated

4
well-known
disgraceful
infamous
_____

6
heinous
famous
monstrous
_____

7
sublime
_____
well-known
celebrated

8
Your vocabulary is
_____!

26 assiduously

(uh-**sid**-joo-uhss-lee) adverb

Long fingernails. Blech! I assiduously trim mine.

What It Means

With care and persistence

How to Use It

My dad hopes to be a magician. He *assiduously* practices his tricks.

More About It

⇄ *Antonym*   carelessly

steadfast

(**sted**-*fast*) adjective

What It Means

Firm and steady
or not changing

How to Use It

We are *steadfast* supporters
of our football team.

More About It

⊜ *Synonym* loyal

I am steadfast in my adoration of animals.

aloof

(uh-**loof**) adjective

What It Means

Distant and not friendly

How to Use It

Lane is so *aloof* that no one gets a chance to know him.

More About It

 Antonym extroverted

Don't ignore Shane. He isn't aloof; he's just an introvert.

volatile

(**vol**-uh-tuhl) adjective

What It Means

Someone who is volatile has rapid mood changes

How to Use It

Theo's *volatile* temper made his friends uneasy.

Watch out. Mr. Cooper gets volatile if you play on his front lawn.

More About It

= *Synonym* excitable

resilient

(ri-**zihl**-yuhnt) adjective

I fall down. I get up. I fall down. I get up. I fall down. I get up. I must be resilient. (Or just clumsy!)

What It Means

Able to handle any situation

How to Use It

My granddad is *resilient*. He went sailing just a week after his fall.

More About It

● *Synonym* flexible

Activity Sheet

A movie director needs help picking actors for his next movie. The actors below are famous for their personalities. Match them with the movie role that would be just perfect for them.

1. **A Loyal Soldier**

   He is firm and steady.

   He Is not likely to change.

2. **A Mysterious Stranger**

   No one knows him too well.

   He is distant and not too friendly.

3. **An Angry Boss**

   His mood changes all the time.

   He is very excitable.

4. **A Come-From-Behind Boxer**

   He's been up. He's been down.

   He can handle any situation.

5. **A World-Famous Brain Surgeon**

   He's careful and attentive.

   If your brain has problems, you want him!

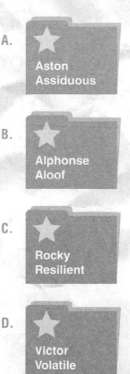

A. Aston Assiduous

B. Alphonse Aloof

C. Rocky Resilient

D. Victor Volatile

E. Sam Steadfast

poignant

(**poin**-yuhnt) adjective

What It Means

Something poignant affects you deeply and makes you feel sadness or regret

A poignant haiku:
She drives me crazy,
but I still really love her.
She is my sister.

How to Use It

The scene where the boy had to put his dog to sleep was really *poignant*.

More About It

＝ *Synonym*   moving

farcical

(farss-uh-kuhl) adjective

What It Means

A funny story in which there are many misunderstandings

How to Use It

The *farcical* movie has one hilarious scene after another.

The <u>farcical</u> juggler pretended to get his shoe stuck in his mouth. He was so funny (and flexible)!

More About It

= *Synonym* silly

prodigious

(proh-**dij**-uhss) adjective

J. K. Rowling is a prodigious writer. I am not. The End.

What It Means

Great in amount or size; very impressive

How to Use It

I love movies with *prodigious* special effects.

More About It

⇄ *Antonym*   paltry

This is one prodigious cucumber!

ruminate

(**roo**-muh-nate) verb

What It Means

To think carefully about something for a long time

How to Use It

Roger was still *ruminating* about the movie two days after seeing it.

What? Take out the trash? I think I'll ruminate on it for a while.

More About It

⊜ *Synonym* ponder

sumptuous

(**suhm**-choo-uhss) adjective

Wow. Your red velvet cape is simply sumptuous.

What It Means

Magnificent and grand in appearance

How to Use It

Movie stars lead very *sumptuous* lives. They have fancy clothes and cars.

More About It

⊜ *Synonym*   luxurious

Activity Sheet

What's your movie personality? Follow the arrows to find out.

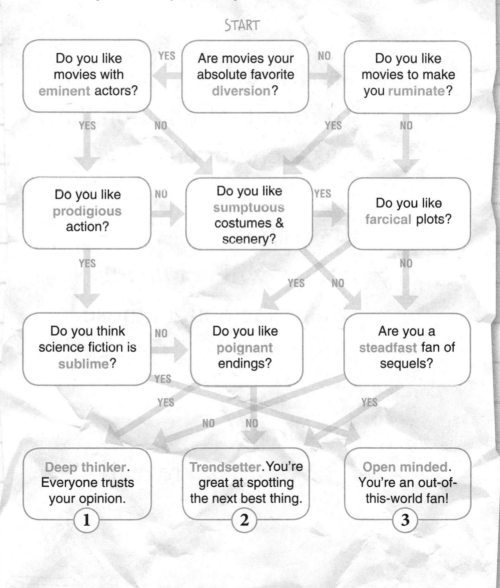

START

Are movies your absolute favorite **diversion**?

YES → Do you like movies with **eminent** actors?

NO → Do you like movies to make you **ruminate**?

Do you like **prodigious** action?

Do you like **sumptuous** costumes & scenery?

Do you like **farcical** plots?

Do you think science fiction is **sublime**?

Do you like **poignant** endings?

Are you a **steadfast** fan of sequels?

Deep thinker. Everyone trusts your opinion.
1

Trendsetter. You're great at spotting the next best thing.
2

Open minded. You're an out-of-this-world fan!
3

divulge

(di-vulj) verb

Tell me! Tell me! Tell me! Please, oh please, divulge the answer to number two.

What It Means

To reveal information that was secret or unknown

How to Use It

Ashley will not *divulge* where she bought those shoes.

More About It

⊜ *Synonym* reveal

Nope. I'm not telling. I will not <u>divulge</u>.

clandestine

(klan-**dess**-tin) adjective

What It Means

Secret, and usually illegal

How to Use It

They were running a *clandestine* business out of their home.

More About It

⇄ *Antonym*   open

Shhh. Top Secret! Don't tell anyone. This meeting is <u>clandestine</u>.

reticent

(**ret**-uh-suhnt) adjective

I'm not really an introvert. I'm just reticent in big groups.

What It Means

Close-mouthed
or not talkative

How to Use It

Ivy is usually *reticent* around
Ellie, who talks nonstop.

More About It

⊜ *Synonym*   silent

furtive

(**fur**-tiv) adjective

What It Means

Sly or sneaky

How to Use It

The man's *furtive* look told me he was up to something.

More About It

≡ *Synonym* secretive

I think Gina wants to go. She keeps making <u>furtive</u> glances at the front door.

surreptitious

(*sur*-ruhp-**tish**-uhss) adjective

The snake was surreptitious as it slithered down the stairs.

What It Means

Secretive

How to Use It

The celebrity made a *surreptitious* entrance through the back door.

More About It

⇄ *Antonym* obvious

Activity Sheet

Use the clues to complete the crossword puzzle. Some of the answers come from earlier sections of this book.

ACROSS

4. A synonym for *reveal*
5. The _____ noise made me cover my ears.
7. Something that is secret and usually illegal
8. An antonym for *obvious*

DOWN

1. A word you can use to describe someone who is unfriendly
2. How you might describe someone who is an introvert
3. A way to describe someone who is sneaky
6. Roy G. Biv, which helps you remember the colors of the rainbow, is an example of this.

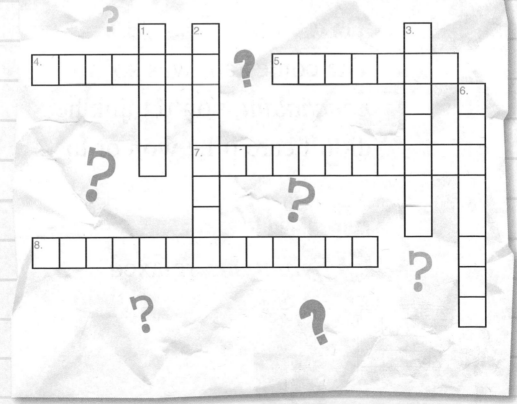

nonchalant

(*non*-shuh-**lahnt**) adjective

I'm really nonchalant about my piano recital . . . . NOT!!!

What It Means

Calm and unconcerned about things

How to Use It

The contestant was so *nonchalant*, you'd think he didn't care if he won or lost.

More About It

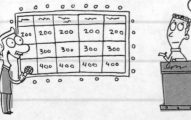 **Synonym** relaxed

complacent

(kuhm-**play**-suhnt) adjective

What It Means

Overly satisfied
with your situation

Don't be complacent.
Vote for Jason.
Change is his aim,
not more of the same.

How to Use It

The singer was so *complacent*
about his fame that he didn't
bother writing new songs.

More About It

⊜ *Synonym*   self-satisfied

Nah... I don't feel like writing today...

pensive

(**pen**-siv) adjective

Think hard. Use your noggin! Dare to be pensive!

What It Means

Deeply thoughtful about something that worries you

How to Use It

Carl was *pensive*. He knew his parents were going to be mad.

More About It

⊜ *Synonym* thoughtful

indignant

(in-**dig**-nuhnt) adjective

What It Means

Upset and annoyed
over something unfair

How to Use It

Ada grew more *indignant* as
she watched the bad TV show.

More About It

⊜ *Synonym*   peeved

Things I say when I'm <u>indignant</u>: No way!
Not fair! You have got to be kidding!
Mom!

forlorn

(for-**lorn**) adjective

I feel forlorn because the frogs have all fled.

What It Means
Sad or lonely

How to Use It
Darra looked *forlorn* as she sat alone eating her oatmeal.

More About It
⇄ *Antonym* joyful

Activity Sheet

It's silly riddles time.. Match each silly riddle with one of the words in the box below.

> indignant nonchalant pensive forlorn complacent

1. What do you call someone who's angry about the big hole in her backyard?

    _____

2. What do you call a snail that no longer cares about his home?

    _____

3. How did the ballpoint feel about making a big decision?

    _____

4. How did Lauren feel after the sad movie?

    _____

5. What do you call a very satisfied secret agent?

    a _____ agent

disparage

(diss-**pa**-rij) verb

Hey, don't disparage my knit scarf. My aunt made it.

What It Means

To speak negatively of something or somebody

How to Use It

I hate to *disparage* you, but that juggling thing is boring.

More About It

⊜ *Synonym*   belittle

extol

(ek-**stohl**) verb

What It Means

To speak admiringly of someone or something

How to Use It

If you *extol* her culinary skills, she'll be sure to make you something delicious.

No one has ever extolled my cooking!

More About It

⊜ *Synonym* praise

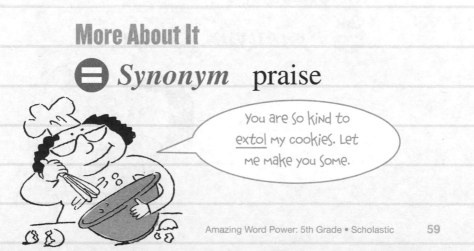

You are so kind to extol my cookies. Let me make you some.

lambaste

(lam-bayst) verb

Note to Self: Avoid being lambasted. Ever.

What It Means

To attack someone harshly with words

How to Use It

The reporter *lambasted* the coach.

More About It

⊜ *Synonym*   criticize

Your team is the weakest we have ever seen. Comment?

NEWS 107

COACH

loathe

(lohTH) verb

Ew! I loathe lima beans. Please don't make me eat them!

What It Means

To dislike someone or something intensely

How to Use It

The bellboy *loathed* days when the elevator was broken.

More About It

⊜ *Synonym* hate

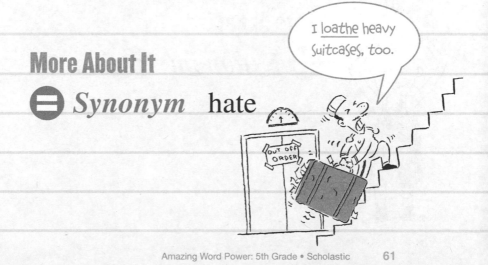

I loathe heavy suitcases, too.

OUT OFF ORDER

kudos

(**koo**-dohss) noun

Kudos to Keisha for becoming class president.

What It Means

Recognition or credit for achieving something

How to Use It

Malik received lots of *kudos* for winning the event.

More About It

 *Synonym* praise

Activity Sheet

Use the clues to complete the puzzle. Some of the words come from earlier sections of this book.

ACROSS

1. Great in size or very impressive
3. Sad
5. To criticize
6. To praise someone
7. To belittle someone

DOWN

1. A synonym for *thoughtful*
2. To dislike someone or something intensely
4. Recognition for achieving something

lethargic

(le-**thar**-jik) adjective

What It Means

Slow or tired

How to Use It

I'm so *lethargic* today I can't keep my eyes open.

More About It

= *Synonym*   sluggish

Monday: peppy. Tuesday: lethargic. Wednesday: hyper. What's up with me?

listless

(list-liss) adjective

What It Means

Lacking in energy or interest

How to Use It

Mia was so *listless*, she spent all day watching TV.

More About It

⇄ *Antonym*   enthusiastic

Listless is like lifeless, right?

sedate

(si-**date**) adjective

Donald = Sedate, good to baby-sit.
Charlie = volatile, no fun to baby-sit.

What It Means

Calm and not hurried

How to Use It

The *sedate* hotel was not much fun for a bunch of kids.

More About It

 *Antonym*   flighty

The Sick Singer gave a very _sedate_ performance.

languguous

(**lang**-gor-uhss) adjective

What It Means

Pleasantly weary

How to Use It

There's nothing like a *languorous* afternoon nap.

More About It

◆• *Related word* languish

Come hang around at my place.
we'll have a languorous weekend.

torpor

(**tor**-per) noun

Torpor = Me in the middle of July.

What It Means

Lacking in mental or physical energy

How to Use It

The scorching weather left us all in a state of *torpor*.

More About It

= *Synonym* inactivity

Activity Sheet

Some animals are real sleepyheads! In fact, one of the animals shown below sleeps more than 20 hours a day. To find out which one it is, put an X in each box with a synonym word pair. Then find a path formed by the spaces you put an X on. You can move up, down, right, left, or diagonally. The path will lead you to the answer. Some word pairs come from earlier sections of this book.

START

lethargic tired	unhurried sedate	lethargic gigantic	sedate volatile	torpor activity
sedate flighty	din noise	sedate excited	heinous kind	nonchalant shocking
languorous weary	calm sedate	nefarious fun-loving	din silence	infamous affluent
torpor inactivity	loathe love	sublime awful	indifferent listless	sedate flighty
slow lethargic	sleepy languorous	aloof unfriendly	bellow whisper	slow lethargic

chipmunk

hippo

snake

mouse

bat

soliloquy

(suh-lil-uh-kwee) noun

Shakespeare wrote a lot of soliloquies.

What It Means

A speech given by one person

How to Use It

The character's final *soliloquy* was very poignant.

More About It

⊜ *Synonym* monologue

loquacious

(loh-**kway**-shuhss) adjective

What It Means

Tending to talk a lot

How to Use It

Carmen and Leah
are both *loquacious*.

I get it. Loqui: means talk. Loquacious is someone who talks a lot.

More About It

⊜ *Synonym* long-winded

eloquent

(el-uh-kwuhnt) adjective

Everyone liked my eloquent speech about the environment.

What It Means

An expressive, clear, and persuasive way of speaking

How to Use It

She is so *eloquent*, it is no wonder she was re-elected.

More About It

⊜ *Synonym*   articulate

colloquial

(kuh-**loh**-kwee-uhl) adjective

What It Means

Colloquial language is language used in everyday informal conversation

How to Use It

We expected her to give a formal speech, but instead it was very *colloquial*.

Hey! check out word 18. Can you find the colloquialism on that page?

More About It

⇄ *Antonym*   formal

Howdy!

circumlocution

(sir-**kuhm**-loh-**kyoo**-shuhn) noun

What It Means

The use of more words than necessary to express something

> If elected, I promise to have popcorn served in the cafeteria every day except the third day of the week and maybe the first day, although Monday . . .

How to Use It

Erin's *circumlocution* during her election speech left us confused.

More About It

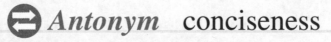 ***Antonym*** conciseness

Have you ever used circumlocution in a book report to make it longer? No? Me neither.

Activity Sheet

What word can help you remember the meaning of the Latin root *loqui* or *locutus*? Use the clues to fill in the correct words below. Then write the boxed letters at the bottom of the page.

1. An antonym of *conciseness*
2. A way to describe someone who talks a lot
3. Language used for informal or everyday situations
4. A synonym for *monologue*
5. A clear and persuasive way of speaking

1. _ _ _ _ _ _ _ _ _ [ ] _ _ _

2. _ _ _ [ ] _ _ _ _

3. _ [ ] _ _ _ _ _

4. _ [ ] _ _ _

5. _ _ _ _ [ ] _

When you see the Latin root *loqui/locutus*, you'll know the word has something to do with

_ _ _ K _ _ G .
1 2 3   4 5

maneuver

(muh-**noo**-ver) verb

watch me maneuver my skateboard along the curb. I rock!

What It Means

To move something carefully into a particular position

How to Use It

How are you going to *maneuver* that big SUV into that tiny parking space?

More About It

💬 *Maneuver* can also be used as a noun.

Big ships can be very difficult to maneuver.

ascend

(uh-**send**) verb

What It Means

To move or go up

How to Use It

The helium balloon *ascended* into the air.

More About It

⊜ *Antonym*   descend

Another A+! I am <u>ascending</u> to the top of the class!

propel

(pruh-**pel**) verb

If I had a super-duper jet pack, I could propel myself into the sky.

What It Means

To drive or push something forward

How to Use It

We decided to *propel* our food across the room. We got in big trouble.

More About It

⊜ *Synonym* thrust

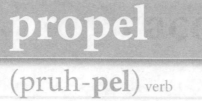

emanate

(**em**-uh-nate) verb

What It Means

To come from or out of something; to cmit

How to Use It

A strange odor is *emanating* from the fridge.

More About It

⊜ *Synonym* spring

Lauren is so groovy. Good vibes *emanate* from her.

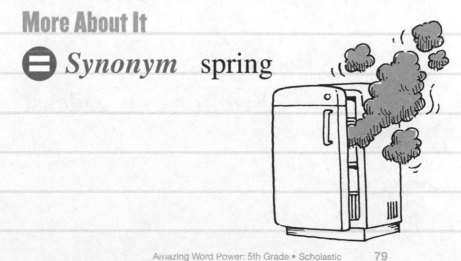

disseminate

(di-**sem**-uh-nate) verb

cover your mouth when you cough! Don't disseminate germs.

What It Means

To distribute or spread something, especially information

How to Use It

My aunts *disseminate* good news very quickly.

More About It

⊖ *Synonym*   broadcast

Activity Sheet

Play the game of Out and Over. Find a word in Box 1 that does not have the same meaning as the other three words. Move that word to Box 2 by writing it on the blank line. Continue until you reach Box 8. Then complete the sentence in that box.

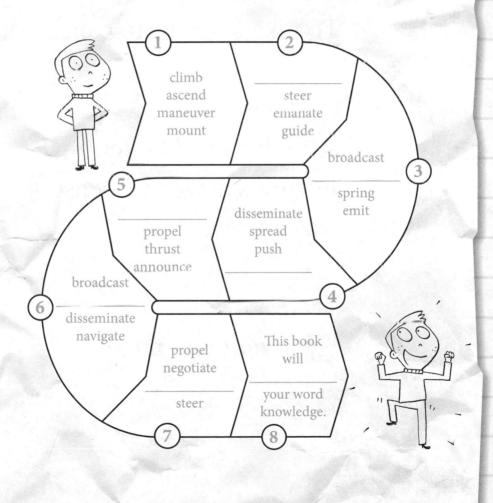

1
climb
ascend
maneuver
mount

2
_____
steer
emanate
guide

3
broadcast
_____
spring
emit

5
_____
propel
thrust
announce

disseminate
spread
push
_____

6
broadcast
_____
disseminate
navigate

4

7
propel
negotiate
_____
steer

8
This book will
_____
your word knowledge.

revoke

(ri-**voke**) verb

My dad revoked my TV time until my grades improve.

What It Means

To take away or to cancel

How to Use It

After his third ticket, Jeffrey's driver's license was *revoked*.

More About It

⊜ *Synonym*   recall

Your license is revoked!

Judge

irrevocable

(ihr-**rev**-uh-kuh-buhl) adjective

What It Means

Unchangeable, or unable to be undone

How to Use It

His terrible concert performance did *irrevocable* damage to his career.

No take backs! That comment is irrevocable.

More About It

= *Synonym* irreversible

Terrible! Awful! Raucous!

I'll never go to one of his concerts again. The critics will lambaste him.

provoke

(pruh-**voke**) verb

My big brother provokes me at least once a day.

What It Means

To annoy someone and make the person angry

How to Use It

My parents think I *provoke* my little sister. I think she screams easily.

More About It

= *Synonym* instigate

vociferous

(voh-**sif**-ur-uhss) adjective

What It Means

Noisy and talkative

How to Use It

A *vociferous* argument broke out between the two drivers.

More About It

 *Antonym* quiet

Hey! Check out word 57. It's a synonym for vociferous.

You're going the wrong way! Turn around right now!

It's your fault! You don't know how to maneuver that thing . . .

70

advocate

(**ad**-vuh-kate) verb

2, 4, 6, 8. Advocate to stay up late!

What It Means

To recommend an idea or a plan strongly

How to Use It

My mom *advocates* for animal rights by writing letters and going to protest marches.

More About It

⊜ *Synonym* support

Activity Sheet

What word can help you remember the meaning of the Latin root *vox/vocare*? Use the clues to fill in the correct words below. Then write the boxed letters at the bottom of the page.

1. To annoy someone or make him or her angry
2. If you're not a careful driver, your license may get _____ .
3. Noisy and talkative
4. If you speak up for something, you _____ for it.
5. A synonym for *irreversible*

1. __ __ __ [ ] __ __ __ __

2. __ __ __ [ ] __ __ __ __

3. __ __ __ [ ] __ __ __ __ __

4. __ __ __ __ [ ] __ __ __

5. __ __ __ [ ] __ __ __ __ __

When you see the Latin root *vox/vocare*, you'll know the word has something to do with __ __ __ __ __ .
 1 2 3 4 5

epidermis

(ep-uh-**dur**-muhss) noun

Nice shorts. Your epidermis is showing!! Ha! Ha! Ha!

What It Means

The outermost layer of skin

How to Use It

After a bad sunburn,
the *epidermis* peels.

More About It

💬 "Dermis" is from
a Greek word
meaning skin.

epidemic

(ep-uh-**dem**-ik) noun

What It Means

A sudden, widespread occurrence of something, such as a disease

How to Use It

The chicken pox *epidemic* lasted for several months.

More About It

⊜ *Synonym*   outbreak

Epi means over, upon, or near. An epidemic is a disease that spreads "over" a lot of people.

You make me sick.

It's not me. It's an epidemic.

73

epithet

(ep-uh-thet) noun

What It Means

An insulting word or phrase

How to Use It

After dropping my lunch tray twice in one week, I earned the *epithet* "klutz."

More About It

 ▶◀ *Related word* epithetic

My epithet for my brother is "worm" because he's always reading. Get it? Bookworm!

epigram

(ep-uh-*gram*) noun

What It Means

A short, witty saying

How to Use It

My favorite *epigram* is, "Always forgive your enemies; nothing annoys them so much."

More About It

⊜ *Synonym*   aphorism

Epigram of the day: I can resist everything except temptation.
                              —Oscar Wilde

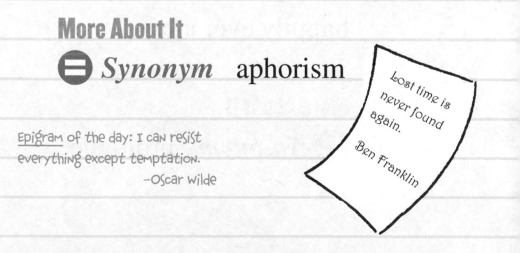

Lost time is never found again.

Ben Franklin

epilogue

(ep-uh-*log*) noun

What It Means

A short speech or piece of writing added to the end of a play, story, or poem

How to Use It

In the book's *epilogue*, we find out that the characters lived happily ever after.

More About It

⇌ *Antonym*   prologue

I have a lot to memorize. I am delivering the play's epilogue.

Activity Sheet

Use the clues to complete the crossword puzzle. Some of the answers are words from earlier sections of this book.

ACROSS

2. My parents are always calm and _____.

4. This is found at the end of a play, story, or poem

7. A sudden outbreak of something, such as a disease

8. Using epithets might instigate, or _____, people.

DOWN

1. To move something carefully into position

3. Your outermost layer of skin

5. A short witty saying

6. A word or phrase that is insulting

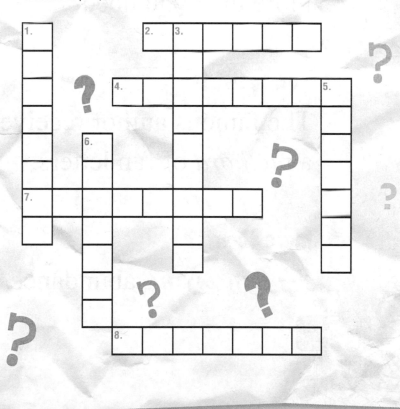

plethora

(**pleth**-uh-ruh) noun

Oooh, my stomach hurts. I ate a plethora of pastries.

What It Means

A large amount of something that is usually more than you need

How to Use It

The famous author received a *plethora* of fan letters.

More About It

 **= *Synonym*** abundance

dearth

(**durth**) noun

What It Means

A shortage of something

How to Use It

The *dearth* of water made it hard to grow tomatoes.

More About It

= *Synonym* lack

There is a dearth of cookies in my house!

pittance

(pit-inss) noun

I bought a new pair of sneakers for just a pittance.

What It Means

A very small amount of something, especially money

How to Use It

How can you expect me to save money when my allowance is a *pittance*?

More About It

⇄ *Antonym* plenty

copious

(koh-pee-uhss) adjective

What It Means

Produced or existing in large quantities

How to Use It

The astronaut took *copious* notes during his space flight.

More About It

⇄ *Antonym*   meager

My mom serves copious amounts of broccoli.

80

profuse

(proh-**fyooss**) adjective

Profuse apology: I'm sorry, I'm sorry, I'm sorry, I'm sorry, I'm sorry, I'm sorry, I'm sorry, I'm really, really, really, really sorry!!!

What It Means

Being or appearing in large amounts

How to Use It

Having to do a *profuse* amount of work makes me cranky.

More About It

≡ *Synonym* plentiful

Activity Sheet

Some new shops are opening up in town, and they need help deciding on names. Read each description below. Then circle the name that you think best fits the store.

1. A toy store with low, low prices

   Ⓐ Toys for a Pittance   Ⓑ A Dearth of Toys

2. A music store that sells instruments and gives music lessons

   Ⓐ A Pittance of Sound   Ⓑ Copious Notes

3. A health food store that specializes in fruit and vegetable juices

   Ⓐ Juice Cacophony   Ⓑ Profuse Juices

4. A cleaning company that guarantees that homes will be dirt-free

   Ⓐ A Dearth of Dirt   Ⓑ Copious Dirt

5. A book store with three floors of books

   Ⓐ A Plethora of Pages   Ⓑ Nefarious Books

gaffe

(**gaf**) noun

Does a half gaffe equal a small mistake?

What It Means

A stupid or clumsy mistake that offends someone

How to Use It

Calm down! You won't get kicked off the team for one small *gaffe*.

More About It

⊜ *Synonym* blunder

catastrophe

(kuh-**tass**-truh-fee) noun

What It Means

A terrible and sudden disaster

How to Use It

Feeding my baby brother turned into a *catastrophe*.

More About It

⊜ *Synonym*   calamity

Running out of jelly is no big deal. Running out of peanut butter is a catastrophe.

egregious

(uh-**gree**-juhss) adjective

No dessert tonight? I find that egregious.

What It Means

Extraordinarily bad or objectionable

How to Use It

Jordan knew playing near the window was an *egregious* mistake.

More About It

= *Synonym* awful

controversy

(kon-truh-vur-see) noun

What It Means

A disagreement that causes a lot of argument

How to Use It

I can understand both sides of the *controversy*.

More About It

⊜ *Synonym*   quarrel

I feel a controversy coming.

Elmwood Road Club house

You must be at least 12 years old to join.

using cell phones at school has become quite a controversy.

debacle

(di-**bah**-kuhl) noun

you + tripping in the lunchroom = huge debacle.

What It Means

A humiliating defeat or failure

How to Use It

Jonathan's attempt to help at the pet store was a *debacle*.

More About It

 Antonym victory

Activity Sheet

Circle the answer to each question. Then write the letters you circled on the lines below. They will spell a very important word to know if you ever make a mistake.

1. Which of these would definitely be a gaffe?

    s) forgetting to thank your best friend for a birthday present

    b) returning a library book one day late

2. Which of these would be an egregious mistake?

    o) not studying at all for your spelling test

    u) skipping one problem on a math homework sheet

3. Which of these is most likely to start a controversy?

    t) opening up a new town swimming pool

    r) banning skateboarding in all city parks

4. Which event could be considered a debacle?

    r) missing a big soccer game because your team had the wrong game time

    w) having your first soccer game of the season end in a tie

5. Which event would be considered a catastrophe?

    x) a cloudy day

    y) a major flood

<u>   </u> <u>   </u> <u>   </u> <u>   </u> <u>   </u>
1   2   3   4   5

vex

(veks) verb

Tying a necktie vexes me.

What It Means

To annoy, puzzle, or frustrate someone

How to Use It

Fixing the computer totally *vexed* Jason.

More About It

= *Synonym* irk

plague

(playg) verb

What It Means

To be troubled by unpleasant things

How to Use It

Celia has been *plagued* by colds all winter.

More About It

 *Plague* can also be used as a noun.

New Rule: Don't let nervousness plague me when speaking in front of the class.

88

agitate

(**aj**-uh-*tate*) verb

what do you get when you agitate my dog, Charley? copious barking.

What It Means

To make someone nervous and worried

How to Use It

We hoped our loud cheers would *agitate* our opponents.

More About It

⇄ *Antonym*   calm

exasperate

(eg-**zass**-puh-rate) verb

What It Means

To annoy or frustrate someone

How to Use It

The man who couldn't make up his mind *exasperated* the waitress.

More About It

 *Antonym*   soothe

My <u>dearth</u> of good grades <u>exasperates</u> my dad.

90

grating

(gray-ting) adjective

I find your violin practicing very grating.

What It Means

Harsh and unpleasant

How to Use It

Bowser's loud barking is very *grating*.

More About It

⊜ *Synonym* irritating

Activity Sheet

Are you easily vexed or agitated? Do some things plague and exasperate you? Do you find these questions grating? Circle the answer to each question. Then write the letters you circled on the lines below. The new word is a synonym for _bug_.

1. Which of the following problems would most likely vex you?

   d) figuring out what you'd like for dinner

   a) fixing a broken remote

2. Which of the following might plague farmers?

   n) beetles and frost

   g) sunshine and water

3. A good way to agitate your parents would be.

   t) to make your bed every morning.

   n) to procrastinate about doing homework.

4. What might exasperate a basketball coach?

   o) a team that can't win

   v) a team that can't lose

5. Which of the following would you find the most grating?

   e) a day without homework

   y) homework on a holiday

___ ___ ___ ___ ___ **is a synonym for _bug_.**
 1   2   3   4   5

truce

(**trooss**) noun

Truces bring peace. Let's advocate for truces!

What It Means

A temporary agreement to stop fighting

How to Use It

Okay, I call a *truce*. We are no longer fighting.

More About It

= *Synonym*   cease-fire

reparation

(*rep*-uh-**ray**-shuhn) <small>noun</small>

What It Means

Help or payment someone gives you for loss or suffering they caused you

How to Use It

As *reparation*, you need to replace the mints you took.

More About It

⊜ *Synonym* compensation

My brother demanded money as <u>reparation</u> for my breaking his skateboard.

serenity

(suh-**ren**-uh-tee) noun

warm bath = serenity; cold shower = grating.

What It Means

Calmness and peacefulness

How to Use It

My parents like the *serenity* of hiking in the woods.

More About It

⊜ *Synonym*   tranquillity

hostility

(hoss-**til**-uh-tee) noun

What It Means

Unfriendly or aggressive behavior toward people or ideas

How to Use It

My mom can't stand any *hostility* between my brother and me.

More About It

 = *Synonym* antagonism

No more <u>hostility</u>! I hereby ban words like hate, <u>loathe</u>, and despise.

eschew

(ess-**choo**) verb

I eschew making games and causing catastrophes or debacles of any kind.

What It Means

To avoid doing something

How to Use It

My brother really *eschews* going to bed.

More About It

= *Synonym*   shun

Activity Sheet

Play the game of Out and Over. Find a word in Box 1 that does not have the same meaning as the other three words. Move that word to Box 2 by writing it on the blank line. Continue until you reach Box 8. Then complete the sentence in that box.

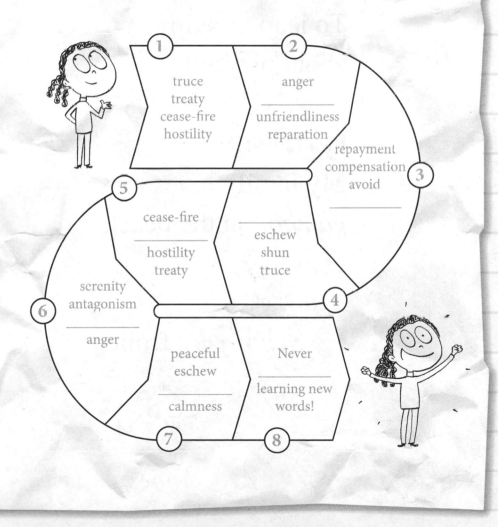

1
truce
treaty
cease-fire
hostility

2
anger
_____
unfriendliness
reparation

3
repayment
compensation
avoid
_____

5
cease-fire
_____
hostility
treaty

4
_____
eschew
shun
truce

6
serenity
antagonism
_____
anger

7
peaceful
eschew
_____
calmness

8
Never
_____
learning new words!

gambol

(**gam**-buhl) verb

I like to gambol in the park.

What It Means

To leap or skip about playfully

How to Use It

My family loves to *gambol* on the beach.

More About It

⊜ *Synonym*   frolic

regale

(ri-**gale**) verb

What It Means

To entertain or amuse somebody, especially by telling stories

I'm feeling loquacious and hilarious, so I will regale you with farcical tales.

How to Use It

Jeremy loves to *regale* us with stories about summer camp.

More About It

 *Synonym*   entertain

convivial

(*kon*-**vi**-vee-uhl) adjective

Our classroom is always convivial because Ms. Rozett is always in a great mood.

What It Means

Enjoyable because of its friendliness

How to Use It

The *convivial* atmosphere at the party made me feel welcome.

More About It

⊜ *Synonym* social

engrossed

(en-**grohst**) adjective

What It Means

Completely involved in something

How to Use It

Brian was so *engrossed* in his book that he didn't see me come into the room.

I got engrossed in a gross show called, "Things That Make You Go YUCK."

More About It

= *Synonym* absorbed

camaraderie

(kah-muh-**rah**-duh-ree) noun

I like you, you like me. That's called camaraderie!

What It Means

A spirit of friendship, especially in a group

How to Use It

Lindy, Mindy, and Cindy enjoyed the *camaraderie* of shopping together.

More About It

⊜ *Synonym*   companionship

Activity Sheet

What's your favorite thing to do on a Saturday afternoon? Keep choosing between pairs to find out. Write your choice for each pair in the box to the right until you get to the last box. Some of the words come from earlier sections of this book.

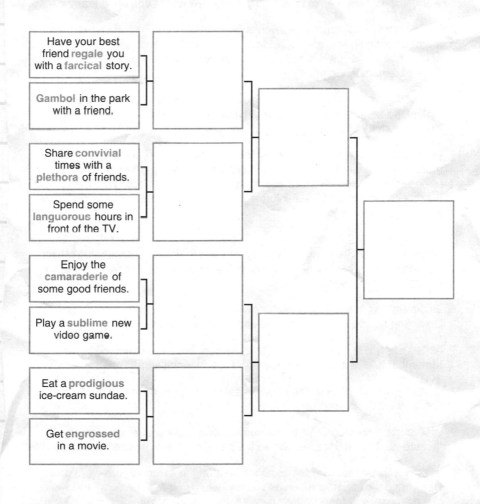

Have your best friend **regale** you with a **farcical** story.

Gambol in the park with a friend.

Share **convivial** times with a **plethora** of friends.

Spend some **languorous** hours in front of the TV.

Enjoy the **camaraderie** of some good friends.

Play a **sublime** new video game.

Eat a **prodigious** ice-cream sundae.

Get **engrossed** in a movie.

Word Power Tips

Are you ready to add 100 words to your vocabulary? Check out the 10 tips below. They're a great way to help boost your Amazing Word Power!

1. **Keep Track of Your Progress.** Use the Checklist that starts on page 125 with the back cover flap to keep track of your growing vocabulary. Cover the definitions with the flap and quiz yourself. (Be sure to use a dry-erase marker.) Test yourself every few weeks to see how many new words you have learned.

2. **Say the Word Aloud.** A pronunciation is given for every word, and you'll also find a pronunciation guide on the inside of the back cover flap. Saying the word will help you remember it better. And the more you say it, the better chance you have of remembering it!

3. **Look at the Illustrations.** Some people remember better when they see a picture, so be sure you look at the illustration included for each word. The illustration may be the key to helping you remember the word's meaning.

4. **Read Each Section of the Word Page.** The more times you encounter a word, the more likely you are to remember it. Each page is designed to give you lots of opportunities to see the word and understand how it is used. The More About It sections include additional information about the words (see the key on the inside back cover flap).

5. **Think About the Word Groups.** How are the words in each group related? Do they share a Latin or Greek root? Are they all ways to describe something? If you can remember what group a word is in, it will help you figure out its meaning the next time you see it.

6. **Do the Activity.** At the end of each group of words, there is an activity page. Doing the activity will help you use and remember the words. Plus, they're fun!

7. **Write Your Own Sentence.** It's true: Using a new word in a sentence helps you to remember it. Try writing your own sentence for each word.

8. **Listen for the Words.** See how often these words come up in conversations, in school, on TV, or in movies.

9. **Look for the Words.** Look for these words online or as you're reading your favorite books or magazines. Make it a game to find them as often as possible.

10. **Use the Words Whenever You Can.** Don't be afraid to exercise your word power! Use your new words as much as you can when you are speaking and writing. You'll amaze your friends, your parents, and your teachers!

1. **reminisce**   reminisce: to think about things from the past
2. **conclude**   conclude: to decide something, based on facts
3. **contemplate**   contemplate: to think seriously
4. **prognosticate**   prognosticate: to predict
5. **mnemonic**   mnemonic: a memory aid
6. **avert**   avert: to turn away or prevent
7. **inadvertently**   inadvertently: mistakenly
8. **diversion**   diversion: something that takes your mind off things
9. **introvert**   introvert: a shy person
10. **convert**   convert: to switch from one idea to another
11. **affluent**   affluent: rich
12. **lucrative**   lucrative: profitable
13. **asset**   asset: something a person or company owns
14. **liability**   liability: money a person or company owes
15. **diversify**   diversify: to get involved in a variety of things
16. **cacophony**   cacophony: harsh sounds
17. **din**   din: a great deal of noise
18. **bellow**   bellow: to shout
19. **raucous**   raucous: rough or loud
20. **melodious**   melodious: pleasant sounding
21. **nefarious**   nefarious: corrupt or vicious
22. **infamous**   infamous: having a bad reputation
23. **heinous**   heinous: terrible and shocking
24. **sublime**   sublime: amazingly wonderful
25. **eminent**   eminent: well-known and respected
26. **assiduously**   assiduously: with care and persistence
27. **steadfast**   steadfast: steady or not changing
28. **aloof**   aloof: distant and not friendly
29. **volatile**   volatile: excitable
30. **resilient**   resilient: able to handle any situation
31. **poignant**   poignant: moving
32. **farcical**   farcical: silly
33. **prodigious**   prodigious: great in size or amount

(Continued on page 127)

Answer Key

Page 9
1. conclude
2. prognosticate
3. mnemonic
4. contemplate
5. reminisce

Page 15
1. introvert
2. fun
3. avert
4. convert
5. diversion
6. inadvertently
TURNED

Page 21
1. rich
2. lucrative
3. asset
4. money
5. liability
6. affluent
7. diversify

Page 27

WHALE

Page 33
The words that move out are:
1. sublime
2. monstrous
3. notorious
4. well-known
5. terrible
6. famous
7. sublime

Page 39
1. E
2. B
3. D
4. C
5. A

Page 45
Answers will vary.

Page 51
Across
4. divulge
5. raucous
7. clandestine
8. surreptitious
Down
1. aloof
2. reticent
3. furtive
6. mnemonic

Page 57
1. indignant
2. nonchalant
3. pensive
4. forlorn
5. complacent

Page 63
Across
1. prodigious
3. forlorn
5. lambaste
6. extol
7. disparage
Down
1. pensive
2. loathe
4. kudos

Page 69

Page 75
1. circumlocution
2. loquacious
3. colloquial
4. soliloquy
5. eloquent
TALKING

Page 81
The words that move out are:
1. maneuver
2. emanate
3. broadcast
4. push
5. announce
6. navigate
7. propel

Page 87
1. provoke
2. revoked
3. vociferous
4. advocate
5. irrevocable
VOICE

Page 93
Across
2. sedate
4. epilogue
7. epidemic
8. provoke
Down
1. maneuver
3. epidermis
5. epigram
6. epithet

Page 99
1. A
2. B
3. B
4. A
5. A

Page 105
1. S
2. O
3. R
4. R
5. Y
SORRY

Page 111
1. A
2. N
3. N
4. O
5. Y
ANNOY

Page 117
The words that move out are:
1. hostility
2. reparation
3. avoid
4. truce
5. hostility
6. serenity
7. eschew

Page 123
Answers will vary.

34. ruminate	ruminate: to think carefully for a long time
35. sumptuous	sumptuous: magnificent and grand in appearance
36. divulge	divulge: reveal
37. clandestine	clandestine: secret, usually illegal
38. reticent	reticent: not talkative
39. furtive	furtive: sneaky or secretive
40. surreptitious	surreptitious: secret
41. nonchalant	nonchalant: calm and unconcerned
42. complacent	complacent: overly satisfied with yourself
43. pensive	pensive: thoughtful
44. indignant	indignant: upset and annoyed
45. forlorn	forlorn: sad or lonely
46. disparage	disparage: to speak negatively
47. extol	extol: to speak positively
48. lambaste	lambaste: to criticize
49. loathe	loathe: to dislike intensely
50. kudos	kudos: praise
51. lethargic	lethargic: slow or tired
52. listless	listless: lacking in energy
53. sedate	sedate: calm
54. languorous	languorous: pleasantly weary
55. torpor	torpor: lacking mental or physical energy
56. soliloquy	soliloquy: monologue
57. loquacious	loquacious: tending to talk a lot
58. eloquent	eloquent: a clear way of speaking
59. colloquial	colloquial: informal language
60. circumlocution	circumlocution: wordiness
61. maneuver	maneuver: to move something into a position
62. ascend	ascend: to go up
63. propel	propel: to drive something forward
64. emanate	emanate: to come out of something
65. disseminate	disseminate: to distribute or spread something
66. revoke	revoke: to take away or to cancel

(Continued on page 129)

Index